# Burning whispers

Nikki Nova

BookLeaf
Publishing

India | USA | UK

Presentation by *BookLeaf Publishing*

Web: www.bookleafpub.com

E-mail: info@bookleafpub.com

ISBN: 9789357446686

First edition 2022

# DEDICATION

To my father.

Thank you for making me believe in myself!


To my dear friend Leti.

Thank you for the support!


To my muse F.

Thank you for the inspiration!

## Come love!

Before the moon and stars
open their eyes,
before the night leaves us with new scars,
come, love, come with the fireflies.

Fly with the wind so warm
to that hill where I am waiting hidden.
Where we can disappear like a storm,
while reaching for moments forbidden.

Our faces the dawn will steal,
without a title our love will be.
Do not ask me who I am, just feel,
read in my look, there is a key.

No, I will not say anything.
I am a secret, just like you.
But we have so much more to bring
to that love, more than we knew.

Come, love, hurry! There is no time.
Come before the sun wakes up,
before I find out that you were never mine,
you were just a dream,
come before my heart breaks up.

# I wanted to tell you three words

I wanted to tell you three words,
my heart to explain with them.
But I couldn't, no one taught me how.

I wanted to give you from my fire,
to keep you warm whilst you wonder around the
world.
But you didn't take even a spark from me,
who can live without a flame?

I wanted to bring you the sun,
but I have had many days without sunshine.
I wanted to sing you the song of the birds
but the melody I forgot.

I wanted to teach you how to dance,
to make you hear the music.
I wanted to show you different ways,
I wanted...

I wanted to tell you three words,
my heart to explain with them.
But I couldn't,
I never knew how.

## She is the sun

A star. Is that what you see?
Look deeper.
Is it shining or is it falling?
Perhaps it is too far.
Will you set me free?
Here is a memory to keep.
The sky is calling.

I wish you knew...
Her madness should be loved.
Yes, she is wild, but she is magic.
She cannot be tamed.
Are you afraid too?
Who wants to be pushed and shoved?
The story could be triumphant or tragic.
Some things cannot be explained.

You see a star.
But she is so much more than that.
She is the sun!
With her touch she can warm you
or she can burn you to dust.
Will you follow her?

In two kind eyes

In two kind eyes
the whole universe I can see.
In two kind eyes
my heart is finally free.

Those eyes - bluer than the see,
deeper than the sky;
from them I shall not flee,
nor can I be shy.

In two kind eyes -
rays of sunshine,
in two kind eyes
I can find the smile of mine.

Like a mirror for my soul
they reflect the magic bright.
In a blink I can lose control,
but even then, I am surrounded by their light.

In two kind eyes
I am in love like a child.
In two kind eyes
I am running into the fire wild.

Who are you?


Who are you standing on my way?
Chasing my sleep away, stealing the laugh from
my lips?
I can see you in the paintings on the wall,
I hear you late at night in my dream.

Your eyes are stabbing me like arrows,
but every sound of your voice is caressing me.
Who are you? Troubling my mind, setting it on
fire?
Are you faith or an illusion?

But my trusting heart is singing –
a bird in blooming garden,
singing and calling you "my love ".
And enchanted I am whispering:
-Here, take my hands and take me away!

## Run away


Run! Run away from me!
Save yourself.
And save me too.
Turn that screaming thought into silence.
Subdue my madness for you.
This madness...
It is scary, it is wild, it is dangerous.
Today – the sweetest warmth,
tomorrow – it can spread like fire into our souls
and turn them into ashes.
I am saying run but actually
I am holding out my hands "stay in my day "...
How am I supposed to run away from myself?
You are all, all a part of me.

The mysterious door


You were to me a mysterious door,
the mysterious key I was looking to find,
the one that will let me explore
beyond the most secure gates of your mind.

And I was searching in the strangest places,
there wasn't a stone that I left unturned,
I must have met more than a thousand faces,
and yet, from them there was nothing I learned.

Did I need a magic spell
or perhaps some kind of a trick?
I honestly couldn't tell
and the gates I started to kick.

The door tightened even more,
 in despair I got lost.
Fear spread to my heart's core,
fear colder than frost.

I was standing alone, exposed,
with no key, no spell, no hope.
How could I get what I desired the most?
Like a prisoner tied with a rope.

So, I leaned on the door,
got the handle in my hand.
Why I didn't think of this before?
I was blind to understand.

All that was needed, was a human touch,
the door stands now wide open,
just a little warmth, not much,
that was the secret unspoken.

*** 

13

Do not ask who he is.
He doesn't have a name, nor face.
I created him from loneliness
and I called him неназовим.
I sculptured him with parts of myself.
That way, he will remain immortal.

## Under sun, under snow, under winds

Under the seasons of the world,
under sun, under snow, under winds
we are walking, me and you.
With endless thirst for each other,
we are walking on the earth.

Under sun, under snow, under winds
I am looking to find in you different faces,
but all I discover is you,
just the way you are.
I am looking to find myself,
my hopes, my dreams –
I can see them all in your eyes,
swimming wild and free in the blue lagoons.

Under sun, under snow, under winds,
we keep composing the story of two souls –
bound one to another.

Phoenix


I am a phoenix - dying,
bursting in flames from your touch.
Growing my wings again and flying
to the shore you love so much.

I have died many times before,
turned into ashes.
But I kept coming back for more,
reappeared from burning flashes.

Today I am reborn,
I feel the fire running through my veins.
There is no reason to mourn,
in the dust I have buried all pains.

The world looks different this time,
with you on some far-distant land.
Where I am yours and you are mine,
I don't need anyone to understand.

Waiting for a train


Here you are,
hidden in the fumes,
you are searching for me in hundreds of rooms,
perhaps went even too far.

But you couldn't find me.
Now you are waiting for a train,
hoping that it will take you far away,
hoping I may sit beside you.

Can you recognize me in the crowd?
I have come the last train to board,
and the pain to cut out with a sword.

So many passengers and somehow,
on the platform alone your voice is walking,
and in this instant only your eyes are talking.
Have we become our only destination?

Was it you?

The whispers in the echoes,
the gentle bruises on my body,
the fingerprints all over my heart?
Was it you?
Your name is carved into every one of my bones.
I keep finding pieces of you in places
I didn't even know you've been.
There are these little fragments of time
where I live in between the beats of your heart.
It was you.

# I erased you

I erased you from my heart
like from paper – worthless typing error.
But the page you tore apart,
for your burden you made her bearer.

Through the hole now only wind is blowing,
furious, unforgiving, damaged.
The emptiness of your soul is showing,
like a handful of dust, it got vanished.

It is sad and cruel, and ugly
to say "goodbye " with words like this.
To you – the dream, the love, the hope, my
lovely,
that we created in a kiss.

But you were only dressed like that dream of
mine,
you were only a false resemblance.
So your face faded away with time,
today of it there is no remembrance.
I erased you permanently from my soul.

Like a bird from a cage I escaped
and I felt the freedom in my wings.
Suddenly, I was wide awake,
embracing what the new day brings.

The air has never felt so sweet,
The sun has never been so bright,
I am free the real dream to meet
and a new chapter to write.

Golden poppy

The rain kept pouring down
silently hitting the leaves,
humming a song with a rhythm calm,
the drops sneaked through my window like
thieves.

As they witnessed our kiss,
my heart melted in the middle of the room.
My name from your lips can you release?
In the fire like a golden poppy I bloom.

Slowly undress my soul,
devour my sun; my skin is crawling.
Only your touch can make me again whole
and keep me from falling.
Up in flames we go, you fire breather.

# Eternal kiss

Come with the endless kiss
of our fated bodies.
Come! Like mystery! Like magic!
Come!
Like a star blinding with its shine,
burn me with your fire,
turn yourself into a handful of dust.

A trace in the night sky will stay after us.
And with our light this trace will glow.
The universe will be then changed, brighter,
and our kiss will turn into eternity.

## We drove long and far

25

As the night was drowning in moonlight,
we drove to that city of stones.
We drove long and far
until the past was behind us
and we got to the end of the horizon
where it was just us.
We had only the sand between our toes
and the breaths between our skin.
He taught me how to listen to the waves that
night
and I taught him how to look at the stars.
I reached out and took one for him,
hid it in my pocket, to wait for his wish.
I couldn't help but wonder
if that wish was going to be me.
Because the only one of mine was him.

# Don't go! Do you hear me?

Don't go! Do you hear me?
Don't leave me alone with the night.
Do you believe together in another world we can
be?
That once more we can meet in the blinkering
light?

I think like children in a forest we will get lost,
if we let go of our hands.
Side by side, all the bridges we can cross,
in the desert we can walk on the glimmering
sands.

If you go, I will be calling you,
but will my voice reach you that far?
You will be calling me too...
So stay where we are.

Don't go! Do you hear me?

# Stolen

Stolen moments - bitter and sweet.
Stolen looks - dangerous and innocent.
Stolen rhymes - from the tip of your lips.
Stolen nights - from the sunrise.
Stolen wishes - from the falling stars.
Stolen love. Stolen everything.
A whole world stolen.
From us.
Who stole us away?
Me from you, and you -
from me. Who?

Lost in her depths


Sitting on that pier,
under the sound of the breaking waves,
he got lost in her depths.
She had a whole universe inside her
and stars beneath her skin.
His senses couldn't focus on anything but her.
And even in the night,
he was soaked in sunlight.
She showed him colors
he didn't know existed,
colors not seen in a rainbow.
She was carrying all of them in her smile
and just like this,
she could create the new
in the ruins of the old.
Like an artist.
But she wasn't sure if he can ever be whole,
it would take too many oceans.

# Cold November

All my dreams are dying embers,
here in the cold November.
Your words are echoing away
and the rhymes with me are solely to stay.

Will you give me one drop of kindness?
To help me cure your blindness.
I have pocketful of poems to give,
yet in them, do you believe?

In front of audience of strangers
and in a world full of doubts and dangers,
will you invite me to dance?
We may become true if you would take the
chance.

Don't you see... I always knew,
I'd give up forever to touch you.
You can burn me alive with that kiss,
and still, even a moment with you – I don't want
to miss.

The road leading to you


Long was the road leading to you,
it took most of my life.
For hundred years I was walking too,
with heartless winds on a constant strife.

I passed through corners sharp and scary
shadows,
almost drowned in raging rivers.
But at last I reached the blooming meadows,
where I met your look and sank in shivers.

Long was the road leading to you,
so long that when you were finally in front of
me standing,
I recognized you behind the eyes blue,
but myself - barely, like ink on old paper -
fading.

From sorrows I've become so thin,
you could read me to the bottom;
see the rain through my transparent skin,
do I remind you of autumn?

Long was the road leading to you
and only for a heartbeat of time we met.
Even if I knew...
The same long road to you I would take.